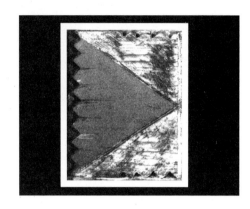

Early NEW MEXICAN FURNITURE

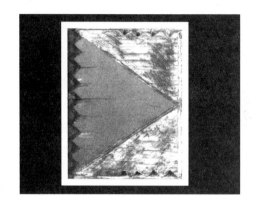

Early NEW MEXICAN FURNITURE

A HANDBOOK OF
PLANS AND BUILDING
TECHNIQUES

KINGSLEY H. HAMMETT

Fleetwood Press

SANTA FE, 1999

This book is dedicated to the beauty, the mystery, the people, and the landscape of New Mexico. ✠

First edition
Printed in the United States of America
10 9 8 7 6 5 4 3 2 1

Book Design by Molly McCord

Photographic Credits:
Dick Francis: pp. 8, 28, 30, 32, 34, 36, 38, 42, 44, 46, 48, 50, 54, 56, 58, 66, 80, 82, 84, 86, 92
Mary Peck: pp. 24, 26, 40, 52, 60, 62, 64, 68, 70, 72, 74, 76, 78, 88, 90, 94
Robert Reck: pp. 2, 14, 22

Cover photo: Late eighteenth-century carved side chair from Cochiti Pueblo. (The Albuquerque Museum Collection; photo by Mary Peck courtesy the Museum of New Mexico, NMF #219)

Back cover: Trastero collected north of San Juan Pueblo near Alcalde. Built between 1750 and 1775. (The Albuquerque Museum Collection; photo by Mary Peck courtesy the Museum of New Mexico, NMF #217)

The furniture presented in this book came from the collection of Shirley and Ward Alan Minge. The collection, along with Casa San Ysidro, a colonial adobe home the Minge's restored in Corrales, New Mexico, were acquired by the Albuquerque Museum in 1997.

Library of Congress Catalog Card Number: 98-93646
Hammett, Kingsley H.
Early New Mexican Furniture: A Handbook of Plans and Building Techniques, - 1st ed.
Includes index
ISBN 0-9648256-2-7

Also by the author:
Crafting New Mexican Furniture, Red Crane Books, 1994
Classic New Mexican Furniture, Fleetwood Press, 1996

Fleetwood Press
2405 Maclovia Lane
Santa Fe, New Mexico 87505
(505) 471-4549

I decided to assemble this book on early New Mexican furniture to offer woodworkers a guide to a style whose simplicity, humility, and elegance has few rivals. These pieces embody the frugal and unpretentious lifestyle on this rustic frontier where their makers lived in isolation for centuries. Here, among the mountains and plains of central and northern New Mexico, they took locally available materials and crafted unique pieces to meet the utilitarian needs of their time.

In an attempt to promote a better understanding of the history, design, and construction of traditionally made New Mexican colonial furniture, this book offers the skilled crafts-man the accurate dimensions that are so critical to building these pieces to their correct proportions. It provides the details and embellishments that make them uniquely New Mexican. For those who may be interested in producing a piece of early New Mexican furniture in the traditional manner, I offer this book as a guide.

I am grateful to Ward Alan and Shirley Minge for the access to this collection, which was lovingly assembled over fifty years and kept in use, intact and well preserved, in Casa San Ysidro, their colonial adobe rancho in Corrales, New Mexico. Dr. Minge, who shared my vision for the need to provide woodworkers with accurate dimensions to reproduce authentic early New Mexican pieces, welcomed me to their home to photograph and measure the pieces presented in this book. Today the furniture, along with the home, is part of the collection of The Albuquerque Museum.

Acknowledgments

I also want to thank the following individuals without whose generous contributions this book would not have been possible: Donna L. Pierce for permission to use her essay on the history of New Mexican furniture; Dick Francis of Talking Mule Fotos, who took many of the photographs of Dr. Minge's furniture, and Judy Sellers, librarian of the Museum of International Folk Art, who provided me with others taken by Mary Peck; Robert Reck for his photographs of Casa San Ysidro; John Schmelz, who produced the measured drawings; designer Molly McCord; editor Robin Slonager; Peter Scholz and Bill Felong for their preparation of the images; and my wife Jerilou for her unflagging support and encouragement.

TABLE *of* CONTENTS

cont.

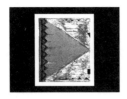

THE HISTORY *of* FURNITURE IN NEW MEXICO
by Donna L. Pierce

If formal guilds existed in New Mexico, their ordinances have not survived. In both Spain and Mexico, master craftsmen often accepted members of their own families into apprenticeship. This practice of keeping a craft within a family was probably continued in New Mexico in an informal manner. As in Mexico, master craftsmen in New Mexico, in at least one instance, trained Indian artisans at the request of the friars, as described by Fray Alonso de Benavides.[1] Benavides also mentioned schools at many of the missions, where Indians were instructed in various crafts, including carpentry, presumably by the friars. Two New Mexican Indian pueblos, Pecos and Cochiti, continued as furniture-producing areas into at least the late eighteenth and mid-nineteenth centuries, respectively.[2]

Introduction

No remaining furniture can be traced to the early part of the eighteenth century. Alan Vedder has suggested that this is "no doubt due to constant reusing and reworking of every piece of furniture until it was literally worn out, as was the case with the tools used."[3] From the later eighteenth century, the furniture forms most common in New Mexico were the same standard forms used in Spain and Mexico – chests, benches, armchairs, side chairs, tables, cupboards, and shelves.

FURNITURE TYPES

✠ CHESTS

As in Mexico and Spain, chests were the most common furniture form used in New Mexico during the colonial period. In inventories of New Mexican estates, the chest is the most frequently listed furniture item, every household owning at least one and some having as many as fourteen.[4] In the New Mexican inventories studied by Taylor and Bokides, more than a third of the chests were imported, mostly from the Michoacan area of Mexico; the rest were of local manufacture.

Three types of chests were constructed in New Mexico; board chests, with six boards joined together by dovetail joints and pegs; framed chests, with panels set into a framework of rails and stiles with pegged mortise-and-tenon joints; and false-framed chests, basically board chests disguised as framed chests by applied strips of molding.[5] All types occasionally contained sections of small drawers in the interior.

The dovetailed board chests were decorated with relief carving created by chiseling away the background area to leave the design raised. Just as these chests have a uniform construction, so they have a standard vocabulary of decorative motifs – rosettes, pomegranates, lions, scallops, vines or branches, birds, circles – in various combinations. Many Spanish Gothic chests were constructed in the same manner: the dovetail joinery being exposed and the background carved away to leave raised patterns of rosettes, fleurs-de-lis, coats of arms, tracery, and geometric designs. This type of board construction with relief design was in use in Spain and Mexico for several hundred years. An example from the seventeenth century exhibits elaborate dovetail joinery and carving depicting the Hapsburg double eagle, vines, and quarter rosettes.

During pre-Hispanic times, a type of lacquerware was produced in Mexico, notably small utensils such as bowls and trays.[6] When the China trade passed through Mexico beginning in the late sixteenth century, oriental lacquer products greatly influenced the production of lacquerware in Mexico. The lacquer industry seems to have reached its peak in Mexico during the eighteenth century, when all types of furniture were decorated in this manner. Areas known for producing lacquerware included Michoacan, Guerrero (part of Michoacan during the colonial period), and Chiapas. An offshoot of the lacquer industry in Mexico was a simplified technique for making inexpensive objects, consisting of designs painted on poorer quality woods (usually pine) that were then covered with a varnish or shellac. The towns of Cuanajo, Michoacan, and Toluca are still known for this type of painted furniture.

These inexpensive painted chests were evidently imported to New Mexico from Michoacan. According to New Mexican oral history, families acquired such chests when their ancestors brought them back from trade fairs in Chihuahua.[7] The chests apparently inspired local artists to paint their own chests and other furniture from time to time.[8] Two board chests from New Mexico are painted with geometric designs and may be the work of Pueblo Indian artists.[9] In his 1776 description of the interior of an Indian home in Tesuque Pueblo, Father Dominguez states, "They usually have... some kind of chest, either plain or painted."[10] The designs on these chests are reminiscent of those on some Pueblo Indian pottery; both the designs and the colors are similar to those on Plains Indian parfleches (traveling pouches).[11] These chests may represent a synthesis of Spanish (both Mexican and New Mexican), Pueblo, and Plains Indian traditions and may indicate a distant influence of oriental lacquerware traditions on southwestern Indian material culture.

✠ CHAIRS

Next to the chest, the chair is the furniture form that appears most frequently in New Mexican estate inventories.[12] Both armchairs and side chairs were made in New Mexico and imported from Mexico. Armchairs made in New Mexico are of mortise-and-tenon construction and are based on the simple lines of the early *sillon de frailero* (priest's chair) of Spain and Mexico rather than the more curvilinear armchairs of the baroque period. Now popularly known as the *sillon de frailero*, these simple rectangular armchairs replaced the hip-joint chair as the most popular type of armchair in Spain around the middle of the sixteenth century.[13] Early *fraileros* were slung with leather or fabric and were collapsible for portability.

Later ones were of solid wood construction and often upholstered with embroidered and fringed velvet or *guadamecil* (a Moorish technique of embossed leather), and were often painted or gilded as well.

These Spanish chairs of mortise-and-tenon construction had slightly raked back posts topped with bracket-shaped or ball finials, narrow arms resting on extended front legs, low side stretchers, and a distinctive high, wide front stretcher often carved or fretted and known as a *chambrana*. One of the most famous examples of a *sillon de frailero* including a fretted *chambrana* is the leather-covered one that was converted into a sedan chair for use by Philip II, now at the Escorial near Madrid.[14] The *sillon de frailero* remained widely popular in Spain and Mexico throughout the seventeenth century and on to the end of the eighteenth century. Beginning in the mid-seventeenth century the legs, side stretchers, and eventually the arms were turned and blocked, reflecting influences from the styles of Louis XIII and Louis XIV, and later were carved and scalloped, reflecting rococo tastes.

Several New Mexican armchairs have wide front and back stretchers reminiscent of the *chambrana* of the Spanish *sillon de frailero*. The stepped geometric patterns on the rails and stile finials of many New Mexican chairs have been related by some authors to Pueblo Indian designs such as the cloud-terrace motif.[15] It should be noted, however, that similar stepped and bracketed designs can also be found on Mexican and Spanish chairs of the sixteenth through the nineteenth centuries, especially in provincial areas, and derive from Moorish prototypes.

Side chairs (*taburetes*) and benches made in New Mexico are similar in construction and decoration to the arm chairs. In some New Mexican chairs, splats or spindles link the stretchers and rails, a construction element common in Spanish and Mexican chairs of the late sixteenth and seventeenth centuries. Several side chairs are decorated with a distinctive gouge-carved design that has been connected to Cochiti Pueblo.[16] Gouge-carved designs can also be found on chairs in Spain and Mexico. A seventeenth century example from Santander in Spain includes back splats, rosette or Romanesque wheel shapes, scalloped stretcher skirts, and overall gouge or chip carving, all

elements found in New Mexican chairs. The cornhusk motifs on the back posts of the New Mexican side chair have been related to Indian designs by Taylor and Bokides.[17]

✠ TABLES

Fixed-leg tables were constructed in New Mexico with a solid framework of four legs with rails or stretchers topped by boards either pegged or nailed to the framework.[18] The Spanish tradition of inserting crosspieces or cleats between the legs and the tabletop was continued in New Mexico into the nineteenth century. On some New Mexican tables splats or turned spindles connect the upper and lower rails. Many New Mexican tables, like their Spanish predecessors, include drawers supported by a central runner between upper rails. Like Spanish tables, New Mexican tables are often decorated with grooves or chip-carved designs on the drawers and rails. The angular scalloping on the rails of some tables is reminiscent of baroque and rococo decoration on Spanish and Mexican tables.

OTHER FURNITURE TYPES

In Spain, cabinets were rare during the Gothic period, but during the Renaissance, when portability was no longer essential, the convenience of the chest-on-chest was recognized. The first use was in church sacristies.[19] Various wardrobes and cupboards evolved from the chest-on-chest. Tall cabinets, know as *fresqueras*, were built in Spain in the seventeenth century and included a spindled top story forming a ventilated food cupboard for storing fruit, cheese, and bread.[20] Large cabinets with wire grille doors are listed in inventories of homes in Mexico in the seventeenth and eighteenth centuries.[21] Tall freestanding cabinets were made in New Mexico of framed construction. Some had solid double doors; others were made with spindles or pierced panels in at least the upper portion of the doors. Most cabinets were constructed with a grooved top section to hold a decorative crest, usually a half rosette or scallop.

Cresting on cabinets became popular in Spain and Mexico in the eighteenth century. According to Burr, heavy cresting is a characteristic of furniture in the Spanish colonies during the eighteenth century.[22] The use of half-rosettes and scalloping on New Mexican cabinets was probably influenced by similar crests on Mexican prototypes. Some New Mexican cabinets have secret or hidden drawers, a motif borrowed from the Spanish *vargueno*.

Among other furniture forms used in New Mexico during the colonial and Mexican periods were two kinds of wooden wall shelves, *repisas* and *alacenas.* The *repisa* was a free-hanging single or double shelf; the *alacena* was built into the adobe wall and covered with double puncheon shutters. Other types of built-in furniture used frequently in New Mexico included adobe benches along the walls, used for sitting and sleeping, and adobe tables along the walls in homes and also in churches, where they served as altar tables.[23] In Spain, built-in furnishings seldom appeared after the Gothic period in the town homes of the wealthy, but they continued in use in the homes of the lower classes and in the provinces.[24] Built-in furniture in adobe homes was also a Moorish tradition.

With the independence of Mexico from Spain in 1821, New Mexico soon became the northern frontier of the new Republic of Mexico rather than the colony of New Spain. The opening of the Santa Fe Trail and trade with the eastern United States introduced new tools, materials, and styles to the New Mexican craftsmen. Occupation by the American army in 1846, the Civil War, and ultimately the arrival of the railroad in the 1880's made the nineteenth century a period of rapid change in New Mexico.

New Mexican furniture of this late period often combines traditional colonial elements with techniques made possible by the availability of milled lumber and new tools, particularly jigsaws and molding planes. Elements of new styles introduced by Anglo tastes and imports, such as Victorian, Queen Anne, American federal, Italian Renaissance, and Gothic revival, were often grafted onto traditional Spanish furniture forms, creating a lively folk style.[25]

SUMMARY

Furniture making in New Mexico during the colonial period was based, in both construction and form, on Spanish prototypes from the sixteenth century. These models were repeated through the years in provincial areas of Spain and in the New World with regional variations. In Spanish furniture, often the construction and form remained constant through several cen-

turies, with only the decorative motifs reflecting changing fashions.

In New Mexico, furniture construction followed Spanish and Mexican prototypes with the exception of the innovative chest-on-legs, which may be a synthesis of two Spanish chests, the *vargueno* and the northern chest with extended stiles. Carved decorative motifs in New Mexico can be traced to Spanish and Mexican predecessors, but the prevalence of certain forms, such as stepped patterns and gouge or chip carving, may also reflect Pueblo Indian traditions. These designs may result in part from the crude tools and brittle wood available in New Mexico, which made the execution of more curvilinear patterns difficult at best. Painted furniture in New Mexico appears to have been inspired by the painted furniture imported from Michoacan, which was in turn influenced by oriental lacquerware. The geometric patterns on two painted chests in New Mexico are probably the work of Indian artists, since they resemble both Pueblo and Plains Indian designs.

In the early colonial period, Indians in the New Mexican pueblos were instructed in carpentry by either Spanish master carpenters or the friars themselves. The apparent absence of formal craft guilds, the geographical distance from Mexico City, and the Spanish Crown's trade restrictions forced New Mexican carpenters to rely on crafts formulas probably passed from father to son. Furniture imported from Spain or Mexico served as models. This artistic isolation probably reinforced the Spanish tradition of grafting new or regional decorative motifs onto traditional furniture forms constructed according to archaic formulas.

Furniture in New Mexico from the late eighteenth and early nineteenth centuries presents a synthesis of elements spanning vast geographical distances, three centuries of time, and various cultures. Some construction techniques and forms date to the fifteenth and sixteenth centuries in Spain and show Moorish influence. Certain decorative motifs can be traced to Renaissance and baroque furniture in Spain and Mexico. Some pieces reflect oriental and American Indian traditions. Whether the furniture was made by Indian or Spanish craftsmen, all of the various influences were tempered by the tools and materials available on the northern frontier of New Spain.

✠ NOTES:

1. Frederick Webb Hodge, George P. Hammond, and Agapito Rey, eds., *Fray Alonso de Benavides's Revised Memorial of 1634* (Albuquerque: The University of New Mexico Press, 1945), p. 67; and Lonn Taylor and Dessa Bokides, *New Mexican Furniture: 1600 - 1940* (Santa Fe: Museum of New Mexico Press, 1987), pp. 14-15.

2. Taylor and Bokides, pp. 9, 18-19, 22, 25, 67, 80-81, 96. Inquisition documents from the 1660s mention Indian carpenters from the pueblos of Sandia, Isleta, Alameda, Jemez, Zia, and Santa Ana. (Archivo General de la Nacion, Mexico City, Tierras, 3268).

3. Alan C. Vedder, *Furniture of Spanish New Mexico* (Santa Fe: Sunstone Press, 1977), p.9.

4. Taylor and Bokides, p. 21.

5. Ibid., p. 23.

6. Teresa Castello Iturbide and Marita Martinez del Rio de Redo, *El arte del maque en Mexico* (Mexico: Fomento Cultural Banamex, 1980); Teresa Castello Iturbide, "Maque," (Artes de Mexico 18, No. 153, 1972), pp. 92-101.

7. E. Boyd, unpublished accession records, Museum of International Folk Art, Museum of New Mexico, A.5.53-36 and A.8.60-1.

8. One of the Valdez chests-on-legs has red, green, black, and white painted patterns outlining the carved designs. This chest is reproduced in color in Taylor and Bokides, p. 35. A board-construction chest in the collection of the Taylor Museum of the Colorado Springs Fine Arts Center has delicate painted designs of scallops, rosettes, plants, and birds in pastel colors. The painting has been attributed to an early nineteenth-century New Mexican folk artist known as Santo Nino Santero. See Vedder, p. 31.

9. Both are reproduced in color in Taylor and Bokides, p. 48.

10. Fray Francisco Atanasio Dominguez, *The Missions of New Mexico, 1776*, Eleanor B. Adams and Angelico Chavez, trans. and eds. (Albuquerque: The University of New Mexico Press, 1976), p. 50.

11. Mable Morrow, *Indian-Rawhide: An American Folk Art* (Norman: University of Oklahoma Press, 1975).

12. Taylor and Bokides, p. 21.

13. Gertrude Hardendorff Burr, *Hispanic Furniture,* (New York: Archive Press, 1964), pp. 26-27; Luis Feduchi, *Historia de los estilos del mueble espanol* (Madrid: Editorial Abantos, 1969), pp. 105-19; Luis Feduchi, *El mueble espanol* (Barcelona: Ediciones Poligrafa, 1969), pp. 102-10.

14. Feduchi, *Estilos,* pp. 65-72; and Feduchi, *El Mueble,* pp. 104-7.

15. Taylor and Bokides, p. 25.

16. Ibid., pp. 96-99.

17. Ibid., p. 99.

18. Taylor and Bokides, pp. 25-26; Vedder, pp. 61-74.

19. Burr, p. 34.

20. For examples, see Burr, pp. 73, 78-79.

21. Manuel Toussaint, *Colonial Art in Mexico* (Austin: University of Texas Press, 1967), pp. 168-69.

22. Burr, p. 107.

23. Dominguez, pp. 62, 106; W.H. Emory, *Notes of a Military Reconnaissance from Leavenworth, in Missouri, to San Diego, in California* (Washington, DC: Wendell and van Benthuysen, 1848), p. 7; and unpublished documents, Archives of the Archdiocese of Santa Fe, New Mexico State Records Center and Archives, Reel 54 (1798 and 1821) and Reel 45 (1818).

24. Burr, p. 22.

25. For examples, see Taylor and Bokides, pp. 119-210; and Vedder, pp.89-94.

Donna L. Pierce is curator of the Spanish Colonial Arts Society and El Rancho de las Golondrinas Museum in Santa Fe.

Excerpted with permission from *The American Craftsman and the European Tradition, 1620-1820,* a catalog produced by the Minneapolis Institute of Arts.

Traditional Details &

DECORATIVE EMBELLISHMENTS

TECHNIQUES *to* RECREATE
TRADITIONAL DETAILS
and DECORATIVE EMBELLISHMENTS

Now Mexican furniture traditionally was made from large ponderosa boards with a few hand tools and certainly no power-driven ones. The most popular joint, and the one most often seen among the pieces offered in this book, was the overlapping through mortise-and-tenon, with a peg to achieve maximum strength and holding power.

Raised panels and geometric designs cut in relief were created with planes and chisels, not routers and plywood guides. The panels floated in grooves cut the length of the piece's legs or door rails and stiles.

To relieve the blank mass of the pine planks, *carpinteros* developed a number of different design details that became recurring themes in New Mexican furniture. Some have their roots in the sacred symbolism of Spain and Europe. Others are drawn from the striking New Mexico landscape and Native American culture. After each detail is described, a piece employing that particular detail is referenced.

Those who have studied New Mexican furniture closely can trace certain details to certain family workshops, so that while a piece may not be signed by its maker, its stamp of origin is often unmistakable. One such case is the Valdez family workshop that was operating in the vicinity of Taos from the late eighteenth century down into the first few decades of the nineteenth. Their work is marked by the distinctive basketweave carving as seen on the Cloud-Top Chair (FW-201). And the often-seen three-step finial on the top back legs of chairs (Step-and-Mesa Chair, FW-207) may be another mark of Valdez work.

How a craftsman held his mortise-and-tenon joints in place is another identifying element. Many used shims in addition to a dowel peg, and they are found in different places: sometimes a single one on the side, other times one on either side, or one on the bottom of the tenon.

I recommend that you recreate these design details in the same way colonial *carpinteros* made them with chisels and gouges. To achieve the best results, take your time and do it the old-fashioned way. If your chisel slips and you cut out a chip of wood, don't worry. It happened to them, too, and that is what gives New Mexican furniture its charm.

Other embellishments may be created with a hand saw, back saw, saber saw, table saw, radial arm saw, or band saw. Take a little sandpaper to the resulting sharp edges to give the piece a softer, rounder look.

The names I have given to these design details are somewhat arbitrary and may not be found in everyone's lexicon. They are used simply to describe the look of the finished detail. Here is how you can create each of them:

DIAGRAMS *of* CARVED *and* GEOMETRIC PROFILES

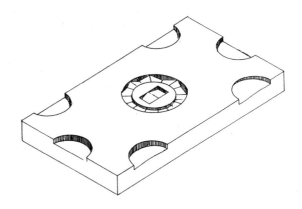

✠ GEOMETRIC RELIEF CARVING

Colonial *carpinteros* used a compass with a sharp trammel point to scratch the half-moon and circular patterns seen in many early chests. An alternative is to score your pattern with a utility knife followed by vertical blows with a sharp chisel. Remove the material to a depth of about 1/8". Holding the chisel almost vertically, come back and clean up any rough edges left by the chisel blows. (see FW-218)

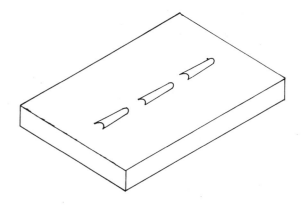

✠ BULLET CARVING

Bullets are created with gouges of varying sizes following a line laid out with a pencil. To make a right-facing bullet, hold the gouge with the concave surface facing to your right and cut into the stock with a single vertical blow with a mallet. Then move the gouge about an inch to the right, and come back to the left with a series of softer taps of the mallet, cutting downward until you meet your first cut. When the chip is removed, the hollowed-out space will resemble the profile of a bullet. (see FW-202)

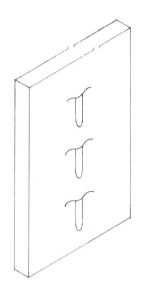

✼ RAM'S HORNS

There are two versions of the ram's horn detail, what some refer to as the cornhusk. The first looks like a single bullet with two horns coming off the top (or an ear of corn with its husk) and is simply made by whacking the gouge down vertically.

In the second version, a series of vertical blows with the gouge are curved into a sweeping pattern. At the bottom of the curve, the gouge blows are set next to each other. At the top of the curve, the pattern switches and the direction of the gouge tip alternates to create an "S" pattern. If you are right-handed, try holding the gouge in your left hand down closer to the point, supporting the tip with your middle and ring fingers, rather than higher up on the handle. You might find you have more control. (see FW-202)

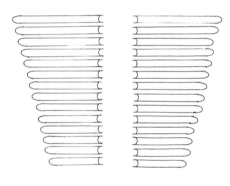

✼ GROOVE AND BEAD CARVING

Traditional craftsmen were always partial to beads and grooves, a task made easier after decorative block planes made their way into the New Mexico Territory following the opening of the Santa Fe Trail in the 1820s. While later pieces used a great deal of the three-bead design, earlier colonial pieces were marked by elaborate profiles cut with hand planes. (see FW-219)

The one-, two-, and three-bead groove was a very popular design detail. I use both single- and triple-bead cutter profile knives set in Delta molding cutter heads in my table saw. (You might also use the Sears #9-3114 molding cutter kit.) A similar effect can be achieved by cutting a kerf with the table saw blade set no more than 1/8" inch high. Cut as many (or as few) parallel lines as you like. For a hand-carved look, you can soften the sharp edges left by the saw blade with a flat chisel.

To make a single bead or groove, take a fairly small radius gouge, cut down about 1/8", and then tap straight and flat the length of bead you want to create. As in carving bullets, some people find they have greater control when pulling the chisel toward them rather than pushing it away. Experiment and see which method you find more comfortable. (see FW-202)

To avoid stripping out an unsightly chip, it may be better to start at the far end of a particular bead and work your way back to the starting point in several smaller segments rather than trying to carve the entire length in one pass. You might carve most of the bead with a mallet and then clean it up working the gouge by hand. Again, experiment and see which works best for you.

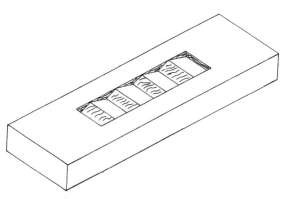

✠ BASKET WEAVE CHIP CARVING

This is actually a series of shallow "V's," one after the other. Start by laying out a 1" wide band down the piece and draw a perpendicular line every inch so the entire strip is divided into 1" squares. Score the outside lines with a utility knife (make two passes to cut deep enough). Then whack at the perpendicular lines with a 1" chisel.

Beginning at the middle of each square, push forward and down with the chisel (with the bevel facing downward) and stop at the bottom of each perpendicular chisel cut. Once you have cut the full length of the piece in one direction, turn the stock end-for-end, and repeat the process so the chisel cuts meet at a shallow "V."

If they fail to meet cleanly, go back and gently work the chisel with a back-and-forth motion of the wrist down the face of the cut until they do. This time, have the bevel of the chisel facing upward. You can clean out any waste caught in the corners with the utility knife.

The end result will resemble a basket weave, particularly when one facet is painted in one color and the opposing facet in a different, contrasting color. Red and blue is one traditional combination. (see FW-201)

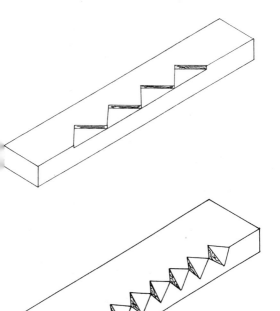

✠ SERRATED EDGE

Lay out the sawtooth pattern along one edge of your stock. With a flat chisel take a whack at each line. Go back and remove each chip to a depth of about 1/8". (see FW-236)

✠ SAWTOOTH CHIP CARVING

Using a sharp utility knife, simply cut and remove a series of "V"-shaped pieces along the edge of your stock. (see FW-218)

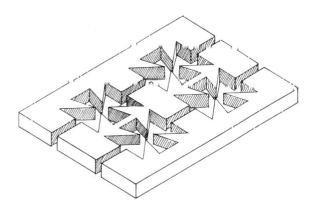

✶ NEGATIVE SPACE

Beautiful effects can be achieved through the use of "negative space," or the pattern that remains after material is removed. One of the most popular patterns is the step-and-mesa (see FW-215). The step-and-mesa design denotes, depending on your source, the profile of the New Mexican landscape with its sharp mesas that sit above the flatter land, the profile of a typical pueblo dwelling or apartment house, or a Pueblo Indian motif that represents the heavens.

If you are creating apron or rail pieces that are not too wide, you can cut this pattern on a radial arm saw with some dado cutters. Begin by taking the piece in which the pattern will appear and ripping it in two. Hold the two halves together and lay out the pattern on the face, along the top, and down the right-hand side of the stack. Remove the material, beginning with the deepest cut first, then raise the saw blade in increments to do the shallower cuts. Larger pieces can be cut with a saber saw or on the band saw. When you put the two halves back together, the light shining through will outline your cutout pattern.

✶ GEOMETRIC DESIGNS

Many other profiles - including the "M" design (see FW-225), the lightning bolt (see FW-236), the bowtie (see FW-206), the tulip (see FW-204), the scallop (see FW-214), the step-and-mesa (see FW-207), and the Cupid's bow (see FW-233) - may be cut with either a power or hand saw. The preferred method is on a band saw or with a saber saw.

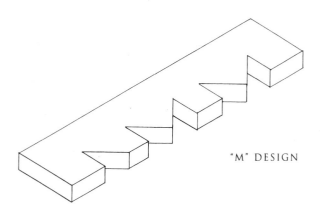

"M" DESIGN

✠ GEOMETRIC DESIGNS (CONT.)

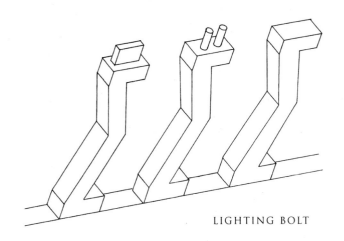

LIGHTING BOLT

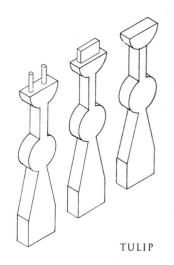

TULIP

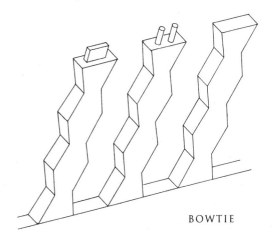

BOWTIE

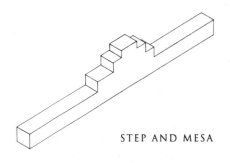

STEP AND MESA

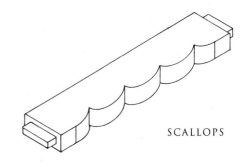

SCALLOPS

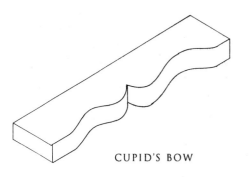

CUPID'S BOW

Photographs &
DIMENSIONED DRAWINGS

CLOUD-TOP CHAIR

𝒯HE STEPS CUT INTO the top of the back legs are similar to those in the Three-Bowtie Chair (FW-206). But the basket weave carving down the front of the legs and the little serrated edges cut into the front edges of the legs indicate that someone took a great deal of care making it. This is the only known chair that can be attributed to the Valdez family workshop, makers of the Chip-Carved Chest (FW-217) and the Chip-Carved Harinero (FW-218), which was active from the 1760s down into the nineteenth century. *Collection of Shirley and Ward Alan Minge (FW-201)*

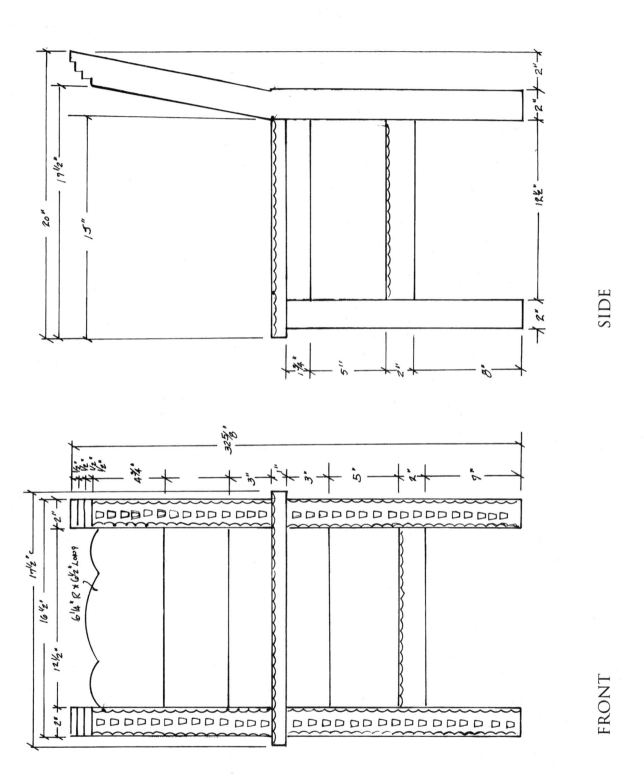

SIDE

FRONT

COCHITI CARVED CHAIR

*B*EADING AND RAMS HORNS decorate the two back rails and front seat rail as well as the top half of the back legs and the front legs. All four legs taper from square to rounds at their feet. The seat on this chair flares from 17 1/4" wide at the back to 19 1/2" in front, beginning 8 1/4" from the back. There is no back seat rail, top or bottom. This particular style of beading and carving is identified with Cochiti Pueblo, and this chair was probably made in the late eighteenth century. *The Albuquerque Museum Collection, formerly a part of the Shirley and Ward Alan Minge Collection (FW-202)*

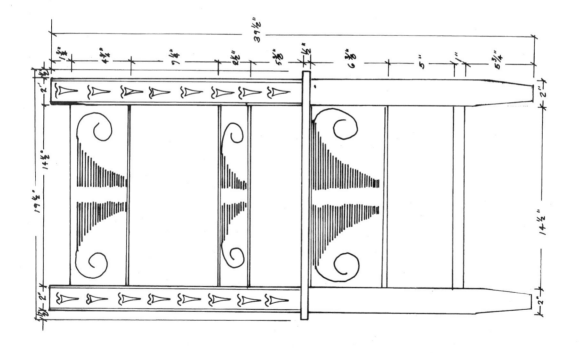

SIDE

FRONT

SLANT-BACK CHAIR

*T*HE UNUSUAL SLANT TO this chair is achieved by a rectangular side rail that meets the back legs 1 1/2" lower than where it meets the front legs. This chair bears a striking resemblance in craftsmanship to the Six-Panel Grain Bin (FW-221) and the Eight-Panel Trastero (FW-228) and were probably built by the same Rio Abajo workshop south of Albuquerque. All reflect the same design elements, like the shallow beading carved with some form of chisel, and each has a very restrained design, much more reserved than that found up north. *The Albuquerque Museum Collection, formerly a part of the Shirley and Ward Alan Minge Collection (FW-203)*

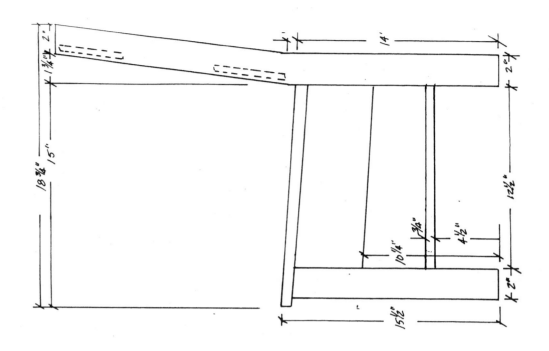

SIDE

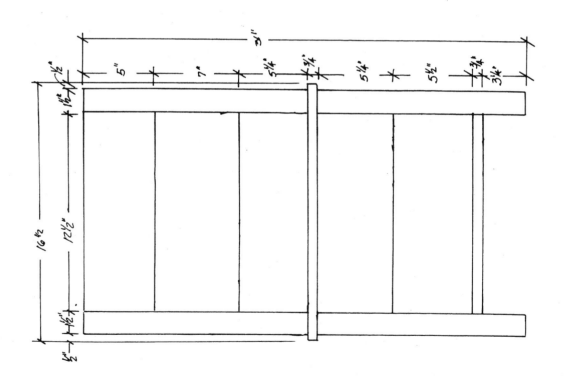

FRONT

29

TULIP CHAIR

*T*HERE ARE THREE STEPS cut into the tops of the back legs and some bead work along the edges of the back rails and the front seat rail. The back splats are each a full and two half tulips, and a chamfer has been cut about 1 1/2" up the front legs. Unfortunately this chair was found after it had been dipped in a lye bath, so there is no telling its original color. It is identical to one in the Colorado Springs Fine Arts Museum that has been dated to 1853. *The Albuquerque Museum Collection, formerly part of the Shirley and Ward Alan Minge Collection (FW-204)*

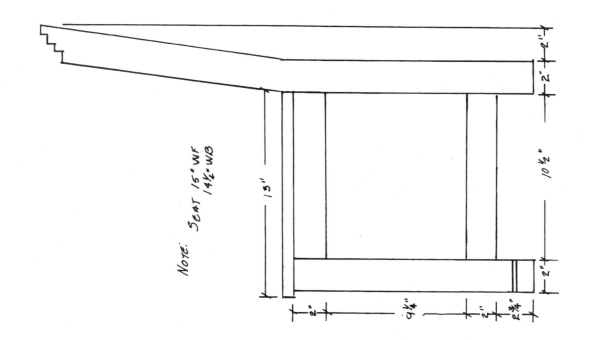

NOTE: SEAT 15" WF
14½" WB

SIDE

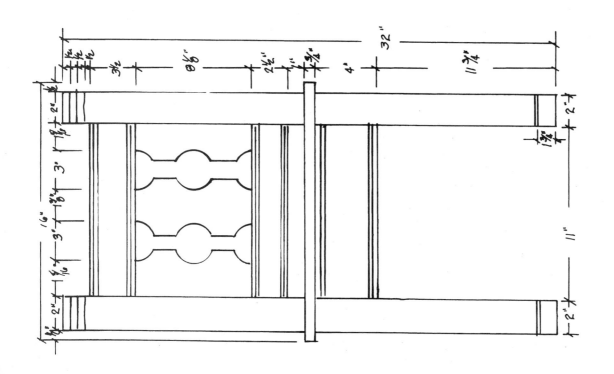

FRONT

31

SINGLE-BOWTIE CHAIR

*T*HERE IS SOME SHALLOW bead carving along the top back rail. The single bowtie is mortised into the top and bottom back rails. While the front seat rail is through-mortise-and-tenoned into the front legs, the side seat rails do not show through. It has round foot stretchers, all of which are through mortise, and the back of the seat does not extend further back than the front of the back legs. This chair is believed to have been built sometime after the Civil War. *The Albuquerque Museum Collection, formerly part of the Shirley and Ward Alan Minge Collection (FW-205)*

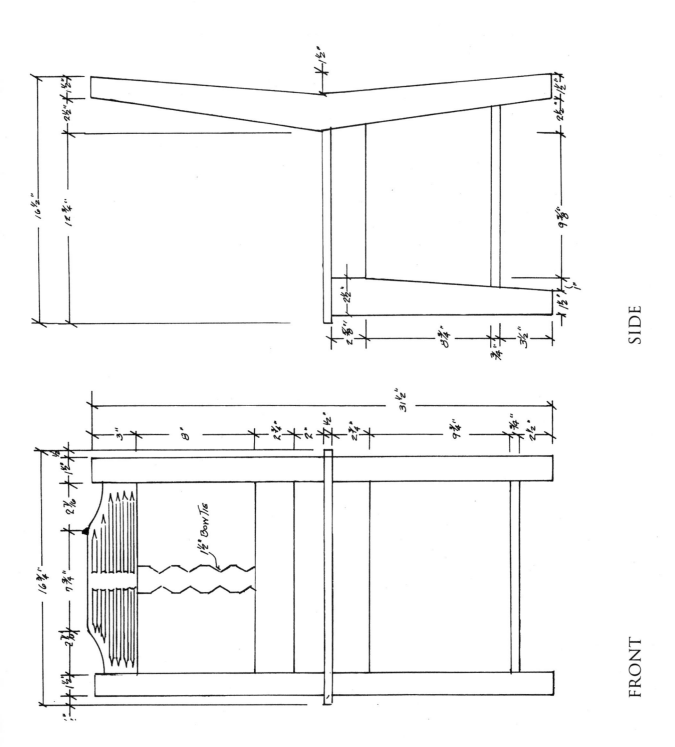

SIDE

FRONT

33

THREE-BOWTIE CHAIR

$\mathcal{F}$OR SOME REASON (or maybe none at all) there is a rectangular design carved into the top and bottom back rails. This chair was originally painted red, and the front legs protrude up above the seat. The step finials on the tops of the back legs may indicate this chair was built in the Valdez workshop. The sweep of the top back rail is reminiscent of the Cloud-Top Chair (FW-201), although this is of a more recent vintage and is not as nicely made. *The Albuquerque Museum Collection, formerly part of the Shirley and Ward Alan Minge Collection (FW-206)*

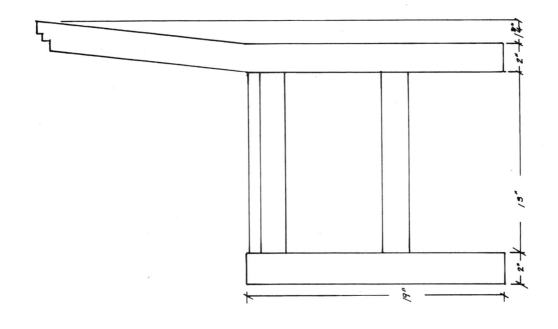

SIDE

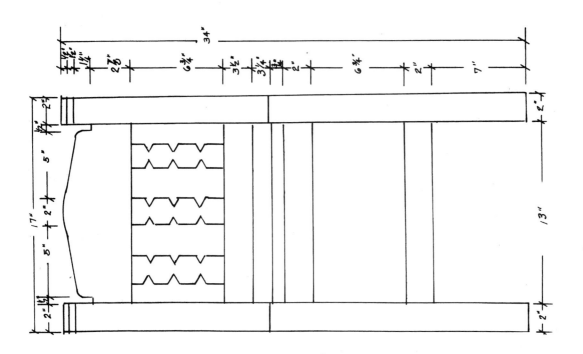

FRONT

35

STEP-AND-MESA CHAIR

𝒯HERE ARE THREE STEPS cut into the tops of the back legs of this chair as well as a mesa design cut into the top back rail, indicating this may have been built under the Valdez influence as well. *The Albuquerque Museum Collection, formerly part of the Shirley and Ward Alan Minge Collection (FW-207)*

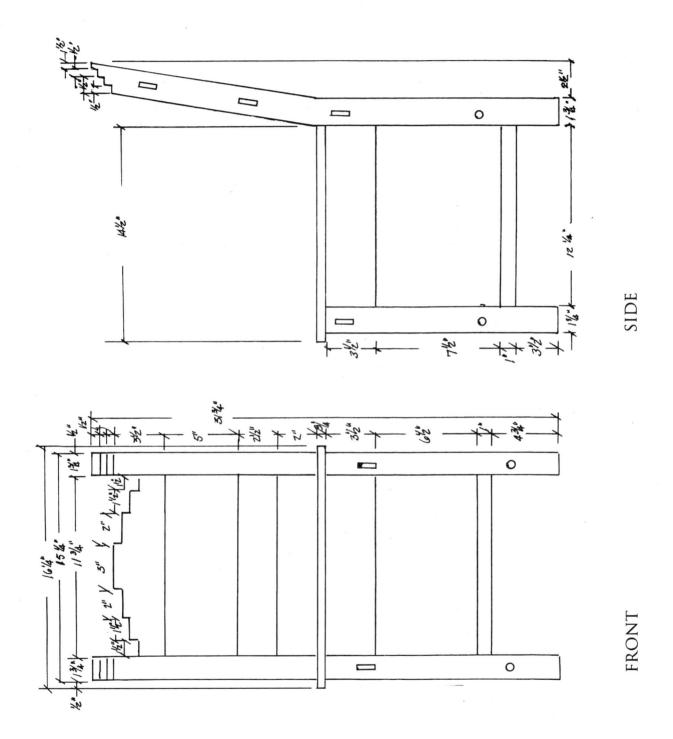

SIDE

FRONT

FINIAL CHAIR

*T*HE LEGS ON THIS chair take some unusual curves and the curve of the top back rail is more or less echoed in the front seat rail. This odd example probably pre-dates the Civil War. Knobs have been found on other pieces of Valdez furniture, but they may not be at all typical of that family's work. Perhaps this was built by someone copying their style or apprenticed to them. *The Albuquerque Museum Collection, formerly a part of the Shirley and Ward Alan Minge Collection (FW-208)*

SIDE

FRONT

SCALLOP-BACK EMPIRE CHAIR

*T*HIS EMPIRE CURVE WAS the New Mexico interpretation of a Grecian-style chair popular in England, France, and the United States in the 1840s. Some people think this type of design goes back earlier than the Civil War, and a few examples of pieces built with milled lumber (like this one) have been dated to that period. This and two similar versions were found in Santa Fe. *The Albuquerque Museum Collection, formerly part of the Shirley and Ward Alan Minge Collection (FW-209)*

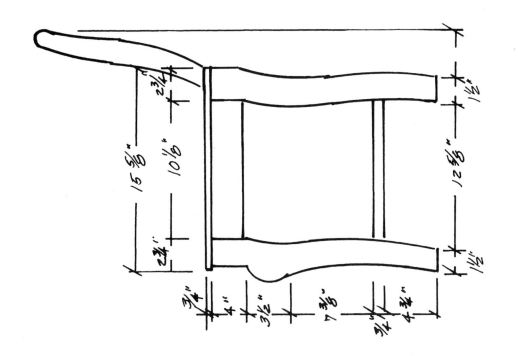

SIDE

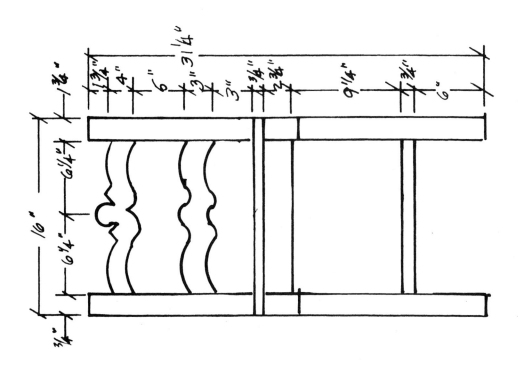

FRONT

HEART-SPLAT CHAIR

*T*HE VERY UNUSUAL HEART-SHAPED back splat is flanked on its sides and bottom by rectangular chip-carved splats. The tops of the back legs are cut into a four-point crown. The front feet have been cut into tapers and the back has a sharp, 6-inch rake. While this chair has all the elements of traditional New Mexico carpentry and joinery, it is an anomaly. A lot of effort was put into it, it has a lot of style, but it was probably made as a special order where the patron had significant input into the unusual design. It begins to look like Eastern furniture, particularly the center splat, while the chip carving in the other splats is typically New Mexican. *Collection of Shirley and Ward Alan Minge (FW-210)*

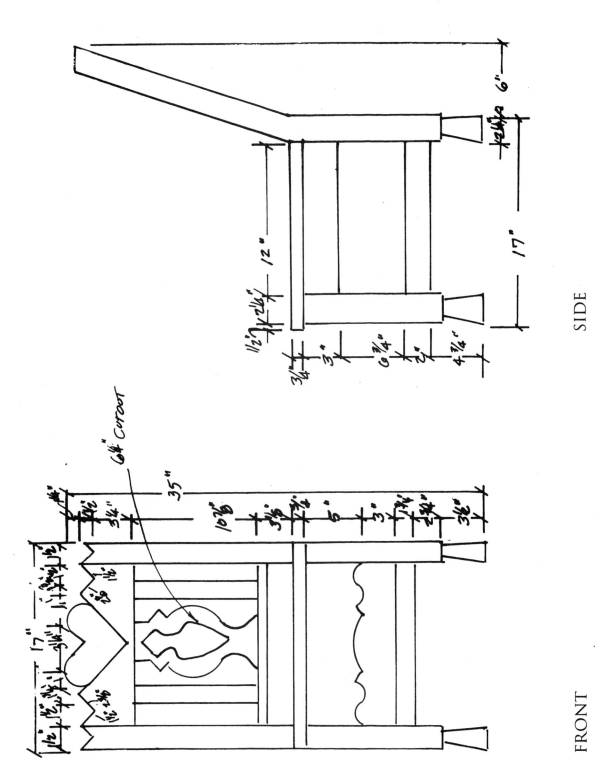

SIDE

FRONT

QUARTER-MOON CHAIR

*T*HE UNUSUAL BRACES BETWEEN the back legs and side rails, let into the back legs with a lap joint, may give this chair added strength. The top of the back rail is cut with a Cupid's bow profile, and simple turnings decorate the three spindles and the front and rear stretchers. The seat tapers from 16 1/2" in front to 14 3/4" at the rear. According to Lonn Taylor (in *New Mexico Furniture: 1600 -1940*), the half-moon bracket is unique and not found on any other New Mexican chairs. This was probably built sometime after the Civil War. *The Albuquerque Museum Collection, formerly part of the Shirley and Ward Alan Minge Collection (FW-211)*

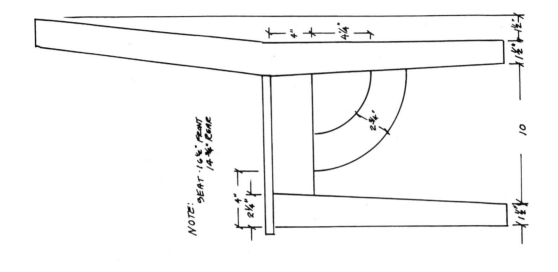

NOTE: SEAT - 16½" FRONT
14¾" REAR

4"
4¼"

4"
2¼"

10

SIDE

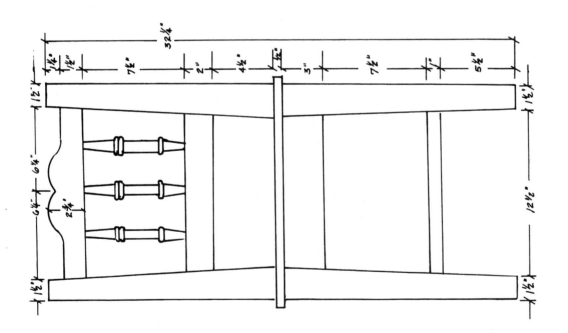

32¼"

1¼"
½"
7½"
2"
4½"
½"
3"
7½"
1"
5½"

6¼"
6¼"
2¾"

12½"

FRONT

45

Benches

PATIO BENCH

𝒯HE LEGS OF THIS simple bench, with feet formed by half-moon cutouts, are mortised up through the top of the seat and set at a slight flare outward. Diagonal bracing has been nailed to the underside of the bench and into the legs for additional stability. This is a very old colonial piece, probably built sometime between 1750 and the 1820s. The window above it, with the little half-moon detail, was probably made by the same workshop that built the Geometric Grain Bin (FW-219). *Collection of Shirley and Ward Alan Minge (FW-212)*

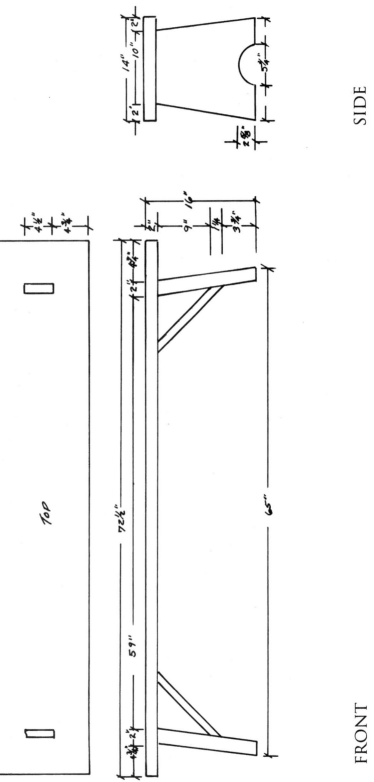

SIDE

FRONT

ADOBE-FLOOR BENCH

𝒯HE FEET ON THIS simple plank bench helped to protect the relatively soft surface of a mud floor. The legs join the seat with a single, wide, through-mortise, and the legs are mortised into the feet. This bench, which may or may not have been used in a church, probably dates from the early nineteenth century. It is believed that the feet were a later add-on because the bench is all hand-made but the feet are milled. *The Albuquerque Museum Collection, formerly part of the Shirley and Ward Alan Minge Collection (FW-213)*

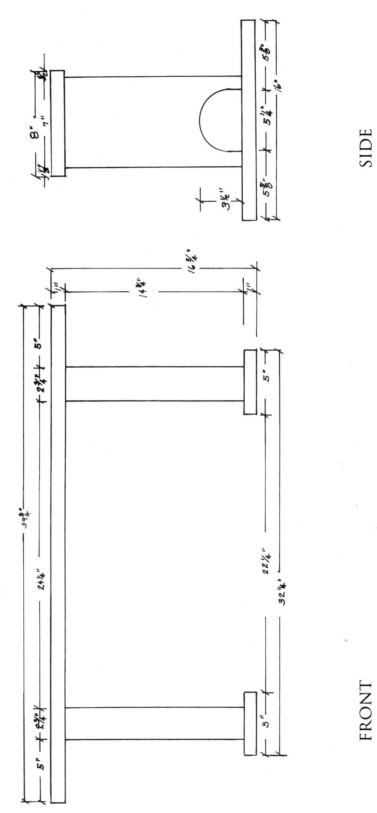

SIDE

FRONT

SCALLOP-BACK PATIO BENCH

*T*HE TOPS OF THE back legs are finished with a carving representing the pomegranate. The scalloped back panel is let into a dado that's been cut into the legs. This bench came from Mora and is missing one of its seat planks. And because it is all hand-adzed, it was probably made sometime between 1750 and 1820. *The Albuquerque Museum Collection, formerly part of the Shirley and Ward Alan Minge Collection (FW-214)*

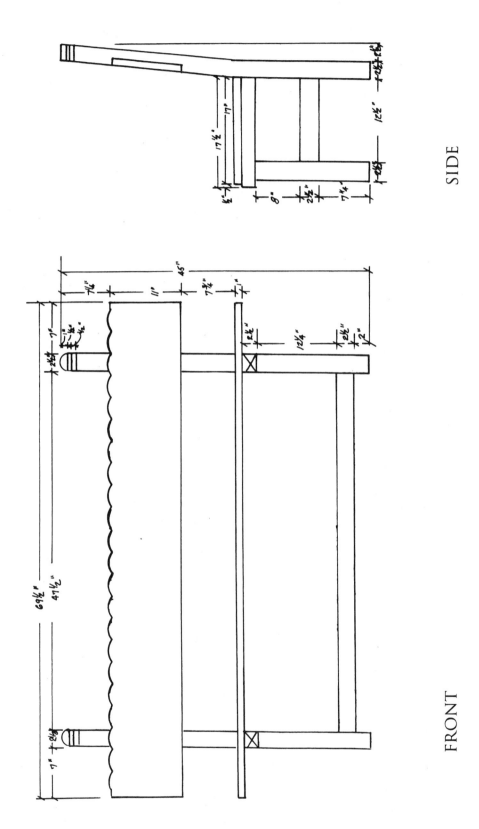

SIDE

FRONT

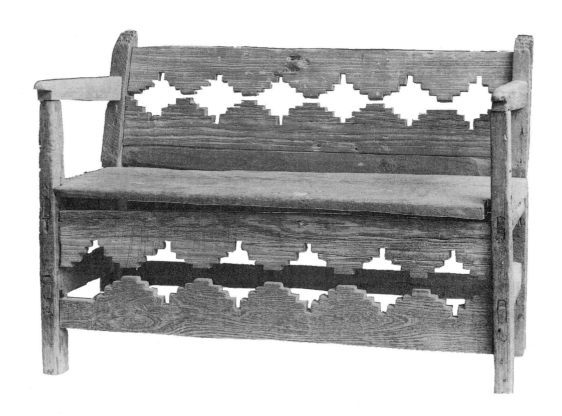

STEP-AND-MESA CHURCH PEW

*T*HIS IS A VERY OLD piece that demonstrates the dramatic effect of a "negative space" step-and-mesa cutout design. It came from Trampas and was most likely built in the late eighteenth or early nineteenth century. *The Albuquerque Museum Collection, formerly part of the Shirley and Ward Alan Minge Collection (FW-215)*

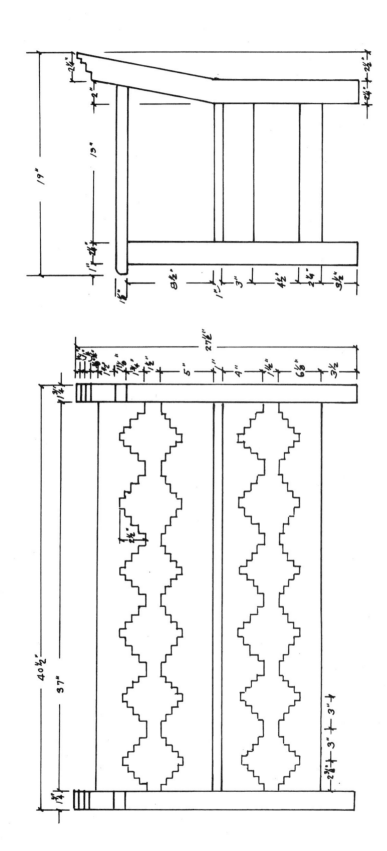

SIDE

FRONT

53

FOUR-SPINDLE CHURCH PEW

𝒯HE TOPS OF THE BACK LEGS, cut with three steps, evidently were added later to the legs that originally stopped at the top of the back rail. The arms are held to the front legs with a through-mortise-and-tenon joint. The seat sits on the two side rails and front rail and is notched around the front leg. There is no back seat rail or back foot rail. All eight spindles are the same and there is a slight kerf in the top and bottom edge of the top back rail, at the bottom of the bottom back rail, at the top of the seat rail, and along the bottom of the foot rail. This pew also came from Trampas, and the turned spindles link it to a lathe operator known to have worked in the Trampas area and on the Trampas church. *The Albuquerque Museum Collection, formerly part of the Shirley and Ward Alan Minge Collection (FW-216)*

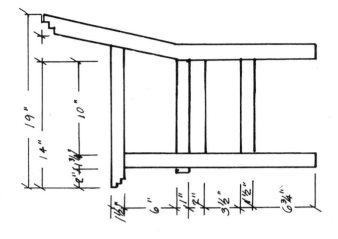

SIDE

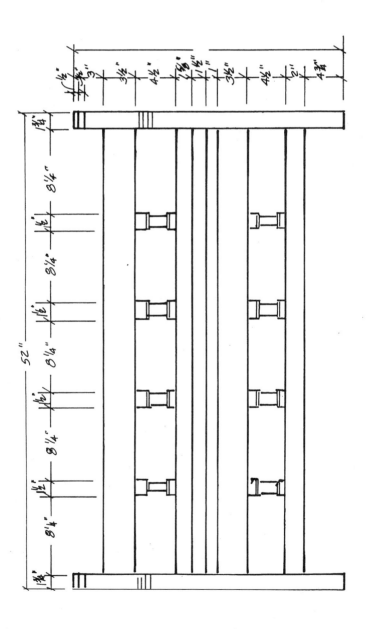

FRONT

CHIP-CARVED CHEST

*T*HE BASKET WEAVE CARVING DOWN the front of legs and along the bottom stretcher, the sawtooth carving around the raised, beveled panel and at bottom of the bottom rail, and the serrated edges cut into the legs (much of which is no longer visible after so many years of wear) tie this piece to others made by the Valdez family. The side and bottom rails are through-mortise-and-tenon, but the top front rail is joined to the front legs with an overlapping joint. The chip carving, which became one of their identifying designs, identifies this as a Valdez piece and links this chest to the Cloud-Top Chair (FW-201). *The Albuquerque Museum Collection, formerly part of the Shirley and Ward Alan Minge Collection (FW-217)*

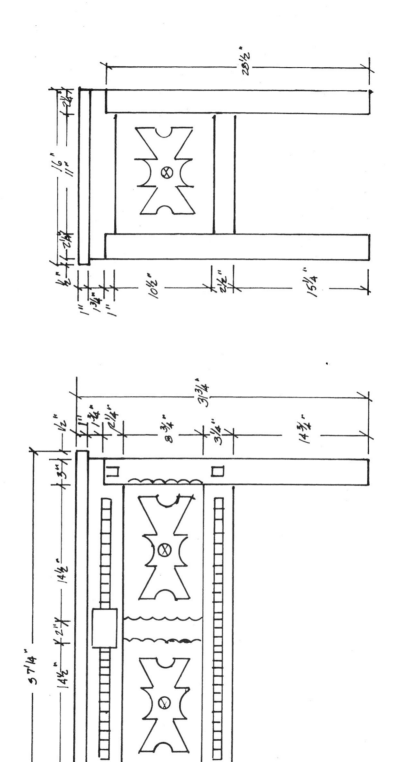

SIDE

FRONT

57

CHIP-CARVED HARINERO

*S*OMEONE TOOK A LOT OF time to carve the eight end panels in the same pattern as the eight found in front. The right side of the top opens (on hinges that have replaced the originals) while the left is fixed. This is another Valdez piece, with their signature design elements – basket weave chip carving, surface darts, and ser-rated edges – and has been dated to around 1800. The angle braces, very typical of the Valdez workshop, were used to stabilize the piece, necessary on one this size. *The Albuquerque Museum Collection, formerly a part of the Shirley and Ward Alan Minge Collection (FW-218)*

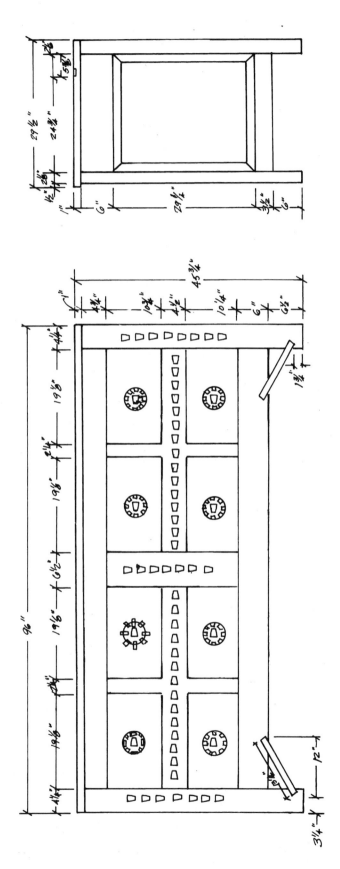

SIDE

FRONT

GEOMETRIC GRAIN BIN

*T*HE HINGED ACCESS HATCH IN the lid of this bin accounts for only the middle third of its top. The front and ends are decorated with half-moon cutouts carved into raised panels that are divided by heavily beaded horizontals and diagonals. The bottom is let into a groove cut into all four bottom rails. The trammel point tool used to cut the half-moon design was brought up from Mexico. This piece was built in Tome about 1800 and is considered one of the most sophisticated and elaborate pieces of furniture to have survived. *The Albuquerque Museum Collection, formerly part of the Shirley and Ward Alan Minge Collection (FW-219)*

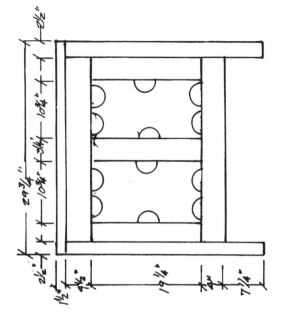

SIDE

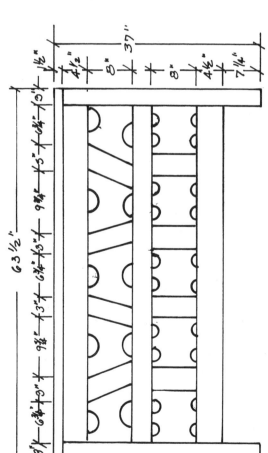

FRONT

LARGE DRAWER CHEST/TABLE

*T*HIS PIECE IS BUILT LIKE a traditional colonial New Mexico table with the top resting on two horizontal bars that are fastened to the tops of the legs. A large drawer slides out on what would be a lower stretcher if it were a true table. This piece came out of a church west of Anton Chico and was made to hold a priest's vestments. It actually shows all the traditional elements of a table. Many of these tables had drawers, but with use have lost them. It's unusual to find a table with its original drawer. *The Albuquerque Museum Collection, formerly part of the Shirley and Ward Alan Minge Collection (FW-220)*

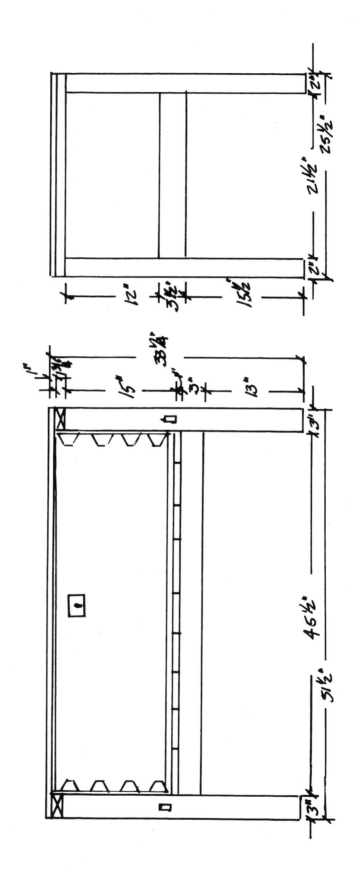

SIDE

FRONT

SIX-PANEL GRAIN BIN

*T*HE SIMPLE DESIGN AND SUBTLE beading on this bin tie it to other Rio Abajo pieces made south of Albuquerque. The top, which is notched around the tops of all four legs, opens on hinges to only half its depth. The bottom is made from eight boards running parallel to the ends that are nailed and pegged to the front and back rails, further supported by a board running lengthwise nailed to the end rails. This very fine piece came from the country around Los Chavez. *The Albuquerque Museum Collection, formerly part of the Shirley and Ward Alan Minge Collection (FW-221)*

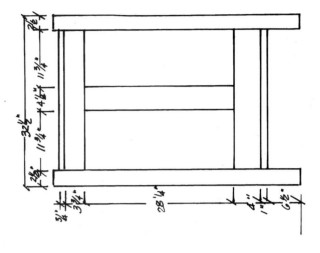

SIDE

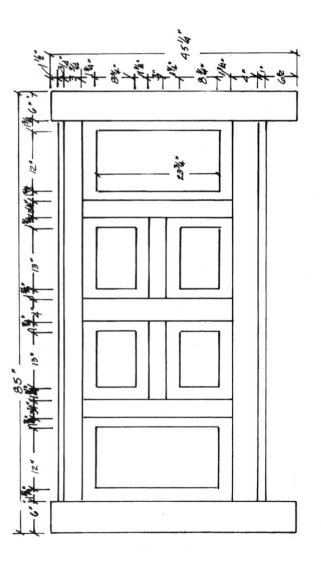

FRONT

STEP-AND-MESA TRUNK

𝒯HE ENDS OF THE LID, which is not hinged but just sits on top of this box, are trimmed in a purely decorative step-and-mesa design. This piece was probably built in the eighteenth century and is unusual for its small size. The decorative ends made it a little dressier for indoor use. *The Albuquerque Museum Collection, formerly part of the Shirley and Ward Alan Minge Collection (FW-222)*

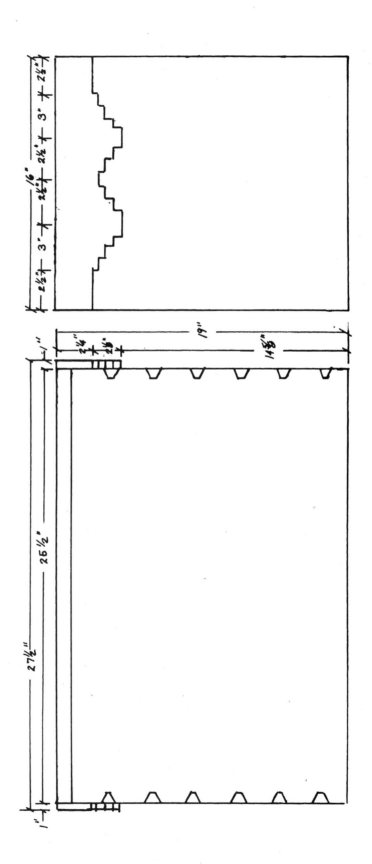

SIDE

FRONT

EMPIRE BUREAU

*C*HESTS OF DRAWERS FIRST MADE their way into the New Mexico Territory with the army in the 1840s. Note that the top drawer extends three inches further out than the bottom two drawers. The very wide top and bottom side rails are set flush with the legs while the end panel is recessed about 1/2". This attempt to copy the Grecian style was probably built before the Civil War. *The Albuquerque Museum Collection, formerly part of the Shirley and Ward Alan Minge Collection (FW-223)*

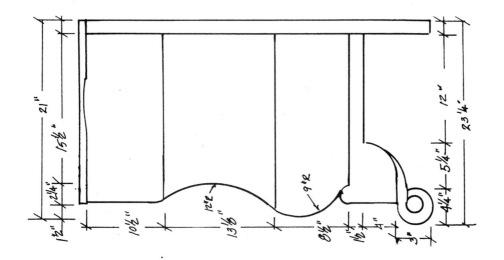

SIDE

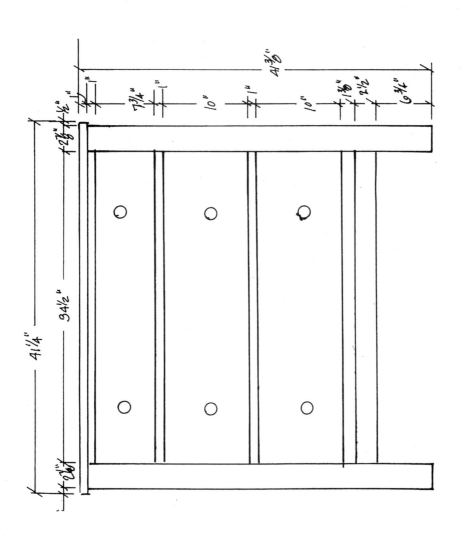

FRONT

"M" DESIGN LIBRARY TABLE

*A*S IS THE CASE WITH so many colonial tables, the drawer for this one is missing. But the runner on which it once slid is clearly visible between the two rails. Note that the "M" design is cut into all six rails. This piece came from Los Chaves, and the "M" design, like that on the Dining Table (FW-225), probably came from the same workshop. *The Albuquerque Museum Collection, formerly part of the Shirley and Ward Alan Minge Collection (FW-224)*

SIDE

FRONT

"M" DESIGN DINING TABLE

𝒯WO ROWS OF THREE-BEAD grooving run above the "M" design in all four rails. The drawer is designed to be flush with the front of the table top and not the rail on which it sits. Close examination shows the scratch marks of the builder's awl that are still clearly visible where he laid out his mortises, cutouts, and carvings. Both of these "M" design tables were probably built sometime between 1800 and 1850. *The Albuquerque Museum Collection, formerly part of the Shirley and Ward Alan Minge Collection (FW-225)*

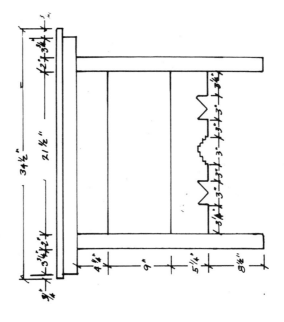

SIDE

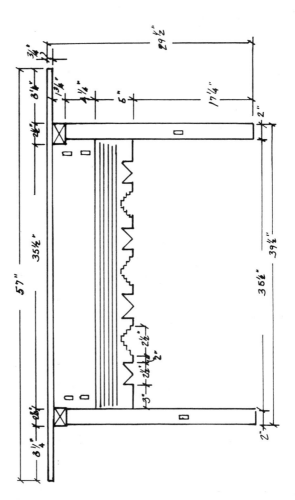

FRONT

WRITING DESK

*W*HILE RAISED PANELS OF EARLIER pieces were decorated with the careful work of the molding plane, later examples, like this writing desk, were embellished with molding that was nailed on. Such is the case with the deeply grooved piece that trims the bottom edge of this desk. This beautiful desk was made after the Civil War and shows definite signs of eastern influence. By then craftsmen were using square nails, commercially made and imported from back East, which first appeared after 1850, as compared to the colonial pieces, which were fastened with wooden pegs. *The Albuquerque Museum Collection, formerly part of the Shirley and Ward Alan Minge Collection (FW-226)*

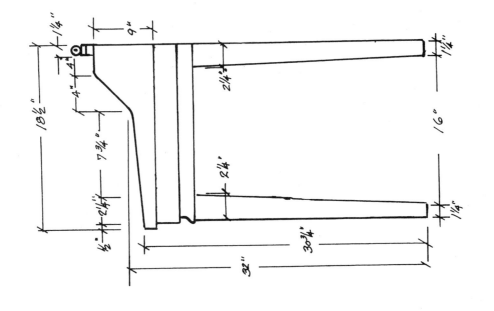
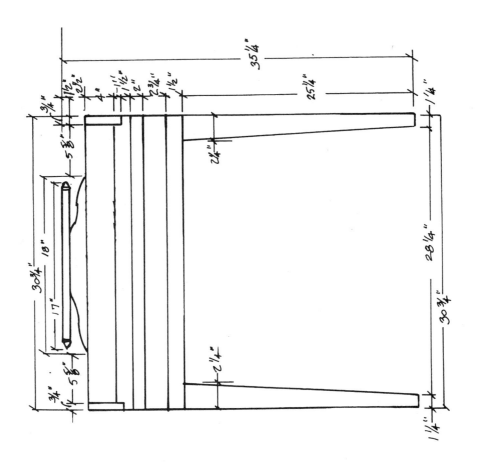

SIDE

FRONT

 *Trasteros*

_____

HALF-MOON TRASTERO

*T*HE LARGE HALF-MOON ENTABLATURE sits in grooves cut into the legs. The doors swing on pintle hinges, and the side rails act as inside shelf supports. The turned spindles date this piece from around 1750 to 1775. It came from the country beyond San Juan Pueblo near Alcalde, and its spindles are similar to those on the Four-Spindle Church Pew (FW-216). This trastero is generally considered one of the finest to have survived in New Mexico.
The Albuquerque Museum Collection, formerly part of the Shirley and Ward Alan Minge Collection (FW-227)

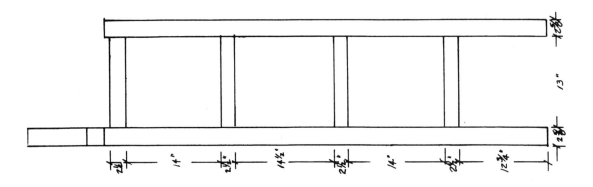

SIDE

2⅛"
14"
2½"
14½"
2½"
14"
2½"
12¾"
13"
24⅛"
2⅛"

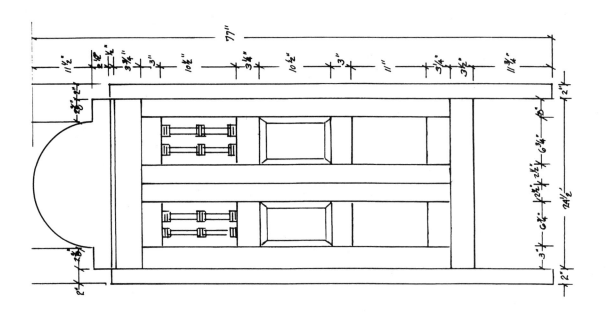

FRONT

77"

11½"
2½"
¾"
3¾"
3"
10½"
3¾"
10½"
3"
11"
3¾"
3½"
11¾"

2½"
2"
12"
6"
6¼"
2½"
2½"
24½"
6¼"
3"
2"

2"
2½"

EIGHT-PANEL TRASTERO

*T*HE SIMPLE CARVING AND INTRICATE panel joinery in this piece mark it as the work of a very skilled carpenter. This is a Rio Abajo workshop piece from Monticello, probably made by the same carpenter family that produced the Slant-Back Chair (FW-203) and Six-Panel Grain Bin (FW-221). All three pieces date from 1750 to 1800. The hand-carved molding and neatly fitted panels on this trastero shows the work of an unusually gifted carpenter and this piece typifies particularly well what is wonderful about New Mexico colonial furniture, including the beautiful hair-pin hinges that still work like new. *The Albuquerque Museum Collection, formerly part of the Shirley and Ward Alan Minge Collection (FW-228)*

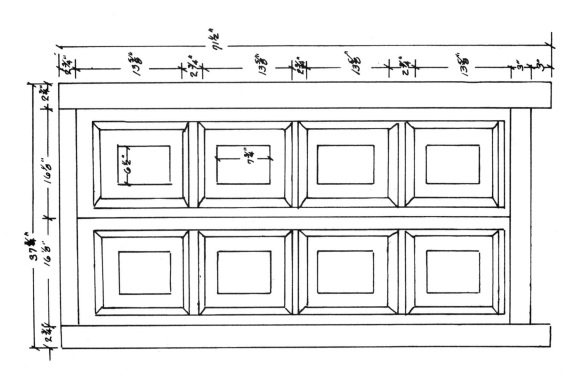

SIDE

FRONT

FINIAL TRASTERO

*T*HE TOP FRONT AND SIDE trim pieces, which float in grooves cut into the legs on this trastero, are decorated with a subtle step-and-mesa design. The edges of the door rails are scored with a three-bead detail. The wrought metal straps fastened with wrought nails appear to be original. The shelves inside this trastero have lovely scalloped plate stops. *The Albuquerque Museum Collection, formerly part of the Shirley and Ward Alan Minge Collection (FW-229)*

SIDE

FRONT

ARROW TRASTERO

*T*HE CURIOUS FEATURE OF THIS piece is the top, which is hinged at the back with pintle hinges and opens to reveal a hidden compartment that is as deep as the top rail. While the door is one long raised plain panel without a bevel, the raised side panels are beveled on all four sides. At one time this piece had a plate stop, a peaked piece that slipped down into the grooves that were cut into the inside edges of the arrows. The door has a typical New Mexico square lock and a wonderful circular pull. Its origin is not known. *The Albuquerque Museum Collection, formerly part of the Shirley and Ward Alan Minge Collection (FW-230)*

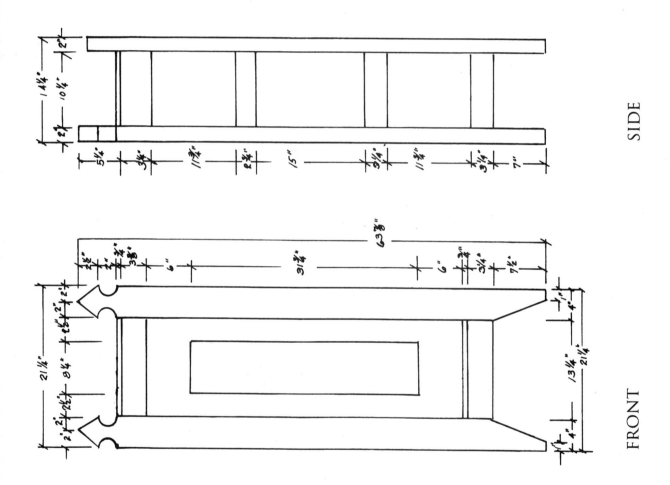

SIDE

FRONT

BAT-WING TRASTERO

𝒯HE SIMPLICITY OF THIS TRASTERO, with sides made from single boards that are held apart with a plain bottom rail and a top rail cut with an unusual geometric design, has made it a favorite of everyone who has seen it. It is a more recent piece, dating from around 1900, and came out of Isleta Pueblo. *The Albuquerque Museum Collection, formerly part of the Shirley and Ward Alan Minge Collection (FW-231)*

SIDE

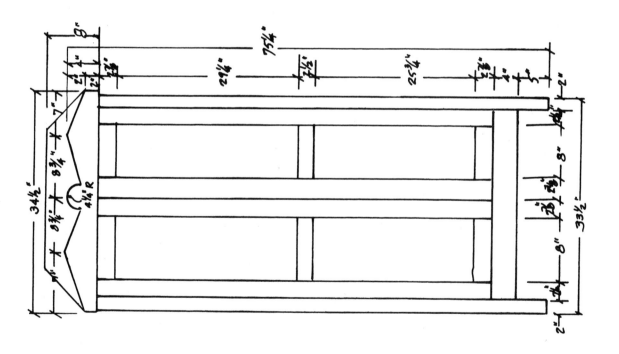

FRONT

CLOUD-TOP TRASTERO

*T*HE FOUR DRAWERS BELOW THE two cabinet doors sit on a base whose top front edge is chamfered. The piece is fairly simple with no carving. The side panels are fastened directly to horizontal mortise-and-tenon side rails that act as inside shelf supports. This trastero was probably built around the Civil War period or just afterward. It's unfortunate that the owner of the antique shop in Santa Fe where it was found thought she could make it look more Hispanic and sell it more easily if she had an iron worker replace the original hinges and leather pulls with these store-bought pulls and butterfly hinges. It was a great mistake. *The Albuquerque Museum Collection, formerly part of the Shirley and Ward Alan Minge Collection (FW-232)*

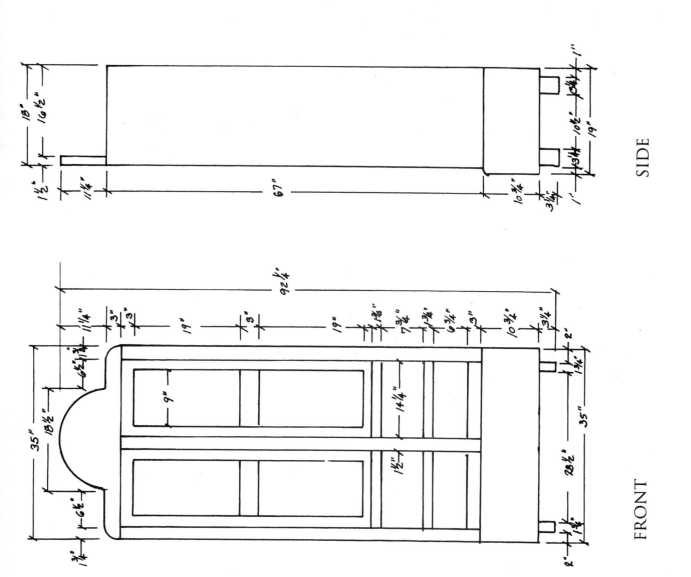

SIDE

FRONT

 *Cupboards*

TWO-DOOR, TWO-DRAWER CUPBOARD

𝒯HIS KITCHEN CUPBOARD IS TYPICAL of the work of Carlos Sena of Bernalillo. The crown molding and stock drawer pulls show how he was influenced by eastern styles. The piece was made from shoe crates that had been shipped from the East across the Santa Fe Trail. Inside you can see, marked in black, that they were addressed to "Bibo Mercantile, Bernalillo, New Mexico." The Bibo store started about 1870, so this was probably made sometime between 1870 and 1880. *The Albuquerque Museum Collection, formerly part of the Shirley and Ward Alan Minge Collection (FW-233)*

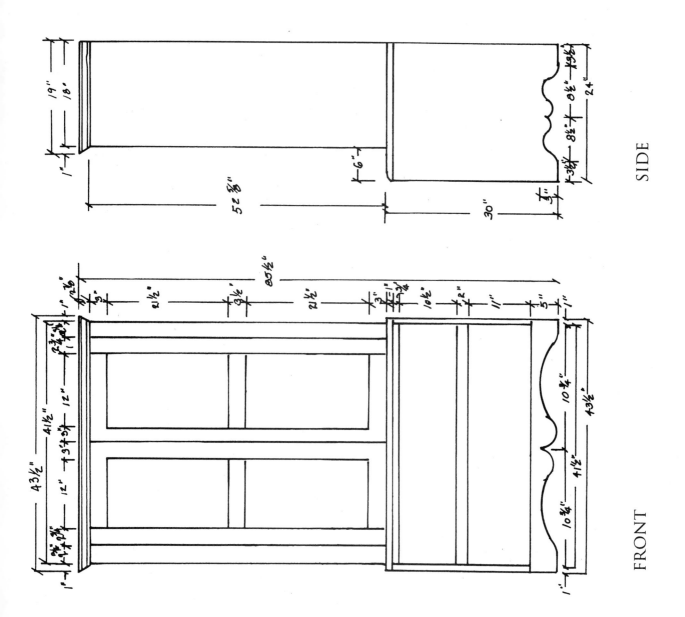

SIDE

FRONT

TWO-DOOR, TWO-DRAWER ROPERO

*T*HIS IS ANOTHER CARLOS SENA piece. He liked the crown moldings and the Cupid's bow design seen at the bottom. This is one of the finest *armarios* found in New Mexico, and also probably dates from somewhere after 1870. Unlike Yankee craftsmen of the time who nailed on decorative molding, Sena carved his into the base of the crown and around the edge of the door rails and stiles. The raised panels front and side are flat without further decoration. When this piece was found it had been stripped of its original paint. But it may have been finished in the prevalent Victorian reddish brown used on so much furniture to imitate the look of mahogany.

The Albuquerque Museum Collection, formerly part of the Shirley and Ward Alan Minge Collection (FW-234)

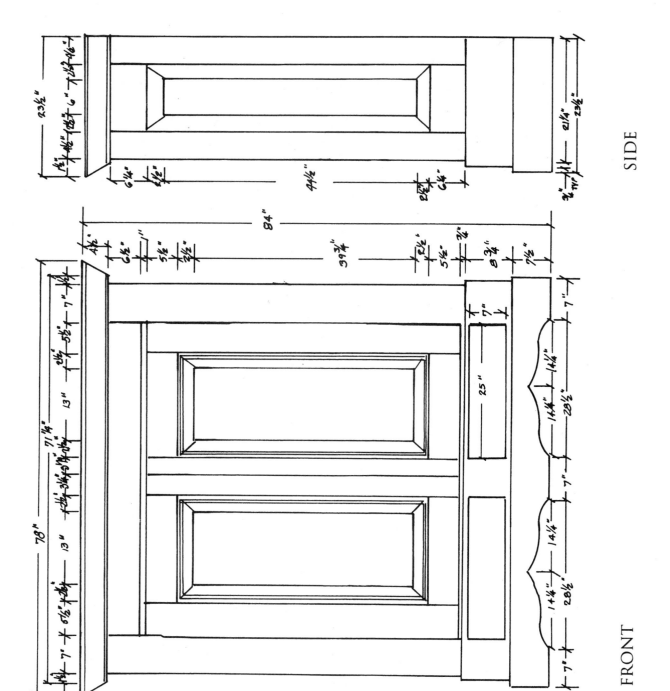

SIDE

FRONT

PIE SAFE

*T*HE NAILED-TOGETHER CONSTRUCTION OF this piece indicates it was probably made after the Civil War. The top and bottom rails and the stiles are simply nailed to the legs. Close inspection reveals that at some point the original end panels were replaced by those with the punched tin inserts. *The Albuquerque Museum Collection, formerly part of the Shirley and Ward Alan Minge Collection (FW-235)*

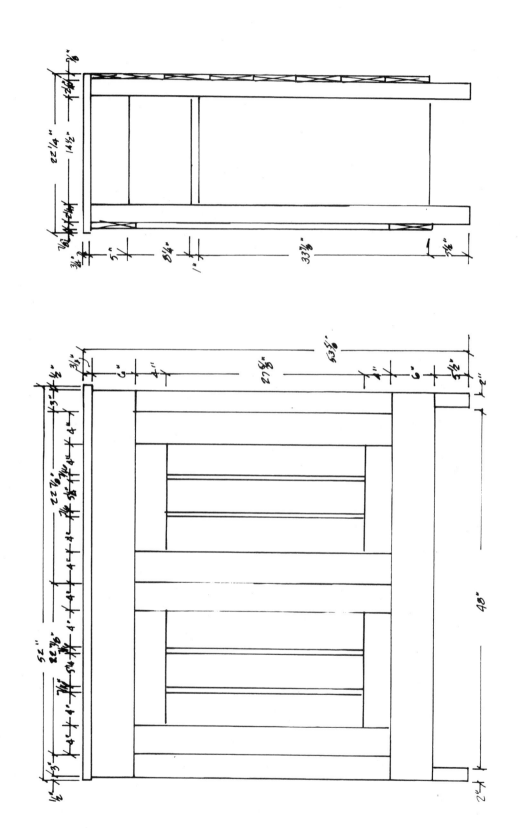

SIDE

FRONT

ALACENA

*T*HE DOORS OF THIS WONDERFUL built-in cupboard have tulips over lightening cutouts over raised panels with serrated edges. These doors, which came out of Isleta Pueblo and date from around 1800, swing on pintle hinges. *The Albuquerque Museum Collection, formerly part of the Shirley and Ward Alan Minge Collection (FW-236)*

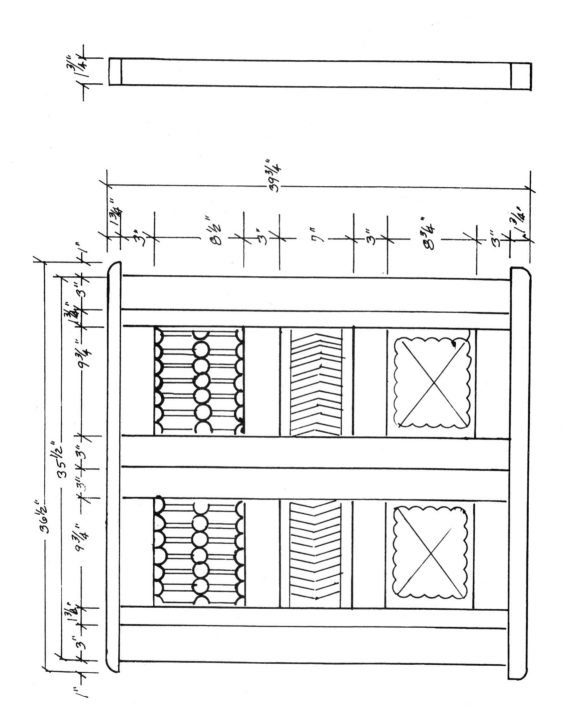

SIDE

FRONT

INDEX